MW00973222

train journey

travel
posters

In the same series

travel posters: sea cruises, olivier frébourg

© Fitway Publishing, 2005
Original editions in French, English, Spanish, Italian

All rights reserved, including partial or complete translation, adaptation and
reproduction rights, in any form and for any purpose.

Translation by Translate-A-Book, Oxford

Design and creation: GRAPH'M/Nord Compo, France

ISBN: 2-7528-0118-1
Publisher code: T00118

Copyright registration: April 2005
Printed in Singapore by Tien Wah Press

www.fitwaypublishing.com

Fitway Publishing – 12, avenue d'Italie – 75627 Paris cedex 13, France

train journeys

jean-paul caracalla

travel
posters

fitway
publishing

Pierre Fix Masseau, © ADAGP Paris 2005

All **on board!**

The earliest railway posters, dating from the beginning of the twentieth century, tended to promote short excursions rather than protracted journeys. Even to this day, taking a train to Mont Saint-Michel, Cabourg or Luchon is, for some people, still fraught with all manner of uncertainties and real or imagined hazards.

Accordingly, the typical early rail travel poster was content to carry images of mountains, beaches and picturesque little villages in the prospective traveller's immediate vicinity. Those intrepid enough to contemplate a journey by rail to Tashkent, Samarkand or Shen-Yang were of an entirely different cast: diplomats, explorers, missionaries or out-and-out adventurers.

The perils of extended travel by rail were largely dissipated with the advent of international express trains, offering the long-distance traveller all the comforts of a voyage by ocean liner. Railway posters now tended to focus less on the ultimate destination than on the notion of 'express' travel, synonymous with comfort, luxury and speed. There was a pronounced shift in graphic design, with quaint and old-fashioned illustrations ceding pride of place to powerful images of the trains themselves, whose names conjured up visions of far horizons.

Unprecedented
scope for adventure

was the image attached to rail travel during the hugely innovative closing years of the nineteenth century: the railways took rivers and mountains in their stride, telescoping distances, bringing nations together, opening up a new era in communications. Their detractors, meanwhile – including academics, writers, politicians and artists – mounted a senseless and ultimately fruitless rearguard action against the railways which would become the future mode of travel par excellence.

'I never travel without my Memoirs. It is always important to have something sensational to read in the train.'

Oscar Wilde

In the wake of the **first** steam locomotive **experiments**

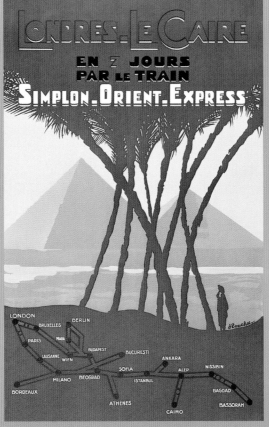

Jacques Touchet, CIWL, © ADAGP Paris 2005

by George Stephenson in the 1820s, it was plain for all to see that the world would effortlessly embrace this new technology and enable hundreds of passengers and thousands of tonnes of freight to be carried easily and efficiently.

'All things considered,
there are only two kinds
of men in this world —
those who stay at home
and the rest.'
Rudyard Kipling

Rafael de Ochoa y Madrazo, CIWL

On 15 July, 1839, an eighteen-carriage train

with no fewer than five hundred passengers travelled the 15.2-mile (24.4-km) stretch from Nîmes to Beaucaire in southern France in an astonishing thirty-six minutes. Vehement opponents of rail travel were up in arms, predicting the direst consequences to travellers' health: it was predicted that moving so quickly from one climatic zone to another could have a deleterious and even fatal effect on passengers, and that the rapid oscillations of the train could provoke hysteria, epilepsy and St. Vitus' Dance. Undaunted by these and other ultimately unsound predictions, the railway pioneers continued to innovate and new lines were rapidly opened. Like progress itself, the development of the steam locomotive was unstoppable.

The name Georges Nagelmackers may have featured less often on posters

than that of his illustrious American counterpart George Pullman, but it is to Nagelmackers that Europe is most indebted for the introduction of comfort in rail travel. Nagelmackers came from a celebrated Belgian family that had produced industrialists, financiers and politicians, but the ambitious young man elected to make his name in another sphere entirely. In 1868, at the age of twenty-three, he left for the United States and criss-crossed the country by rail, discovering in the process that the railway sleeper cars designed by George Pullman could make rail travel a pleasure rather than a necessary evil.

Pierre Fix Masseau, CIWL. © ADAGP Paris 2005

'The idea was to climb aboard any old train that would take me from Victoria Station to Tokyo Central.'

Paul Theroux

'If we climb all the steps in Valparaiso we'll have travelled round the world.'

Pablo Neruda

Franck H. Mason, © ADAGP Paris 2005

FLYING SCOTSMAN

200 RESTAURANT CARS
on the L·N·E·R

By 1872,
Georges Nagelmackers
had created

trains equipped with bogies to reduce unpleasant vibration, carriage interiors as luxurious as cabins on board an ocean liner, gourmet dining-cars instead of hit-or-miss station buffets, and onboard services provided by qualified and dedicated personnel. Nagelmackers put this programme together over the space of a few short months, forcing his vision through in the face of determined opposition. His Compagnie Internationale des Wagons-Lits expanded rail travel all over Europe, becoming the conveyor of Europe's royal families and the creator of the renowned Orient Express.

'My true passion is to know and to feel and that passion will never be stilled.'

Stendhal

Henri Folart, PLM

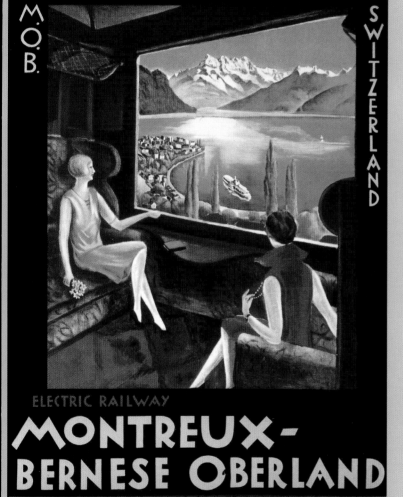

'What is important
is not to see different
countries but to see them
through different eyes.'
Anon.

'Roam the world and
turn your back politely
on the burden years of
study.'

Samuel Beckett

THE ELECTRIC
ST. GOTTHARD LINE
SWITZERLAND

'If you climb aboard the
wrong train there is no
point in walking back
along the corridor in the
right direction.'
                    Dietrich Bonhoeffer

'I will say nothing,
think of nothing ... but
infinite love will rise
in my soul and, like a
gypsy, I shall go far,
very far, happy as if I
were with a woman.'

Arthur Rimbaud

Pierre Fix Masseau, CIWL, © ADAGP Paris 2005

TOFT
BY RAIL

OR (WITH PARTICULARS OF CHEAP
S STATIONS AND INQUIRY OFFICES

COMP¹e INTERNATIONALE DES WAGONS-LITS
& DES GRANDS EXPRESS EUROPEENS

AGENCES
DE LA COMPAGNIE

Luxury rail travel finds favour with the literati

as demonstrated by the testimony of Valery Larbaud's fictional, compulsive and international express traveller, A. Olson Barnabooth, who professed that he 'experienced for the first time the full sweetness of life while riding in a compartment of the Northern Express between Wirballen and Pskov'.

SUMMER ON THE FRENCH RIVIERA
BY THE BLUE TRAIN

Charles Alo, CIWL.

'Let us make haste then,
head held high, our step
quickening as we travel
all the countries of this
world.'

Seneca

'Through my compartment window I watched the little towns come and go and would happily and humbly have spent my life in each and every one of them ...'

Valery Larbaud

DR, CIWL

Enveloped

by the 'anguished music'

of the *Harmonika-Zug,* the nabob of Valery Larbaud savours the 'nocturnal glide through the lights of Europe' from the sumptuous confines of his mahogany-lined sleeping car (Dominque de Roux, Gallimard Editions, Folio, 1983).

LMS — BY NIGHT TRAIN TO SCOTLAND — LNER
IT'S QUICKER BY RAIL
FULL PARTICULARS FROM LMS OR LNER OFFICES AND AGENCIES.

'How **alone I am,**
he thinks,

'and how pleasant this is, sitting here with my travel trunk on the carpet, my sweet-smelling leather slippers, the heavy brass ashtray, the mirrors and the intertwined initials V.L. …' (Valery Larbaud, *Collected Works*, Bibliothèque de la Pléiade, Gallimard Editions, Paris, 1957).

'A lottery ticket promises
less than a train ticket.'
Paul Morand

The frontiers of **Europe** are non-existent for **Paul Morand,**

French diplomat, author, playwright and poet. Diplomatic immunity and the confines of a railway carriage allowed Morand to become 'like a bird of passage in a moving cage', enjoying his travels across the Balkans, while those around him – deposed princelings, arms dealers, secret agents, doe-eyed madonnas and conspiratorial Ottomans – thronged the corridors of the Orient Express. 'Nothing reminds me more forcibly of my native land than when I climb into this itinerant firebox provided by the Compagnie Internationale', noted Morand in *L'Europe Galante* (one of his many travel books). As he sampled truffles in champagne in the company of fabulously wealthy oriental merchants, his companion, Paul Claudel, confided that these merchants were so careless about their wealth that they even left their diamonds in the baggage car!

'The world is too big
and weighs too heavily,
that's why we plough
head-first into every mad
adventure under the sun.'
Jack Kerouac

PARIS-LYON-MEDITERRANEE

CHEMIN DE FER
DU MONT-BLANC
DE St GERVAIS AU
GLACIER DE BIONNASSAY

ROGER BRODERS

Roger Broders, PLM, © ADAGP Paris 2005

'The real secret of
staying healthy and
happy is to keep the body
moving and the mind at
rest; that's what travel
is all about.'

Vincent Voiture

W. S. Bylitipolas, CiWL

From the very onset of rail travel,

children everywhere have been fascinated by trains. As an adolescent living nearly a century ago in St. Petersburg, Vladimir Nabokov chanced one day across a very special object on display in a travel agent's window on Nevsky Prospekt – a ninety-centimetre long model of an oak-coloured international sleeping car. Nabokov would later write that it mirrored the original 'down to the last detail – a far cry from my own little toys fashioned from crudely-painted tin'.

Vom Reisen mit der Eisenbahn

'Breasts and electric trains are children's toys that men play with.'
Jean Cazalet

'Arrive. On time. Keep going.'
Raymond Carver

Bernard Villemot, © ADAGP Paris 2005

Villemot

une Nuit
EN VOITURE-LIT

SNCF

'I have twenty countries in my mind and the colours of a hundred cities in my soul.'
Arthur Cravan

Bernard Villemot, © ADAGP Paris 2005

EXACTITUDE

ETAT

'But where is it then,
this voyage?'
Henri Michaux

Pierre Fix Masseau, © ADAGP Paris 2005

IL VESUVIO
con
LA FERROVIA E LA FUNICOLARE

'Man always finds
a reason for going
somewhere else.
Saint John Perse

'Of all my books the one I like best is my passport.'

Alain Borer

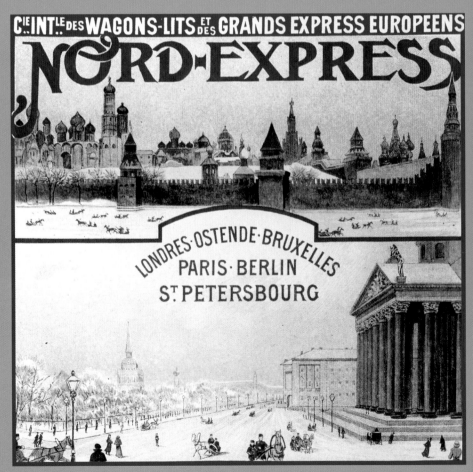

DR,, CIWL

The **memory**
of this beautiful scale
model fired

Nabokov's imagination, prompting the author of *Lolita* to recall his early Wagon-Lits excursions between his native St. Petersburg and Paris, ensconced in the magnificent and magic 'Northern Express'.

'If my memory serves me correctly,' Nabokov would later write, 'I travelled from St. Petersburg to the French capital on at least five occasions, typically *en route* to Biarritz or the French Riviera … My mother and her maid would travel in the coach next to that occupied by my father and myself, and my father's valet, Ossip, would have to share his compartment with a complete stranger'.

'It was at night,' continues Nabokov, 'that the Compagnie Internationale des Wagons-Lits and the Great European Express trains lived up to their name and reputation. From my couchette in the semi-darkness of our compartment, I'd sit and look out, sit and observe …' (Vladimir Nabokov, *Other Shores*, Koch, Neff & Oetinger, 1999). One can picture him there, taking in everything in the carriage around him, and then drifting off to sleep, dreaming he was the engineer.

Never fear life. Never fear adventure. Trust in fortune and trust in fate. Take off. Find new places to conquer, fresh hopes to nurture. The rest will follow in abundance.

Henry de Montfried

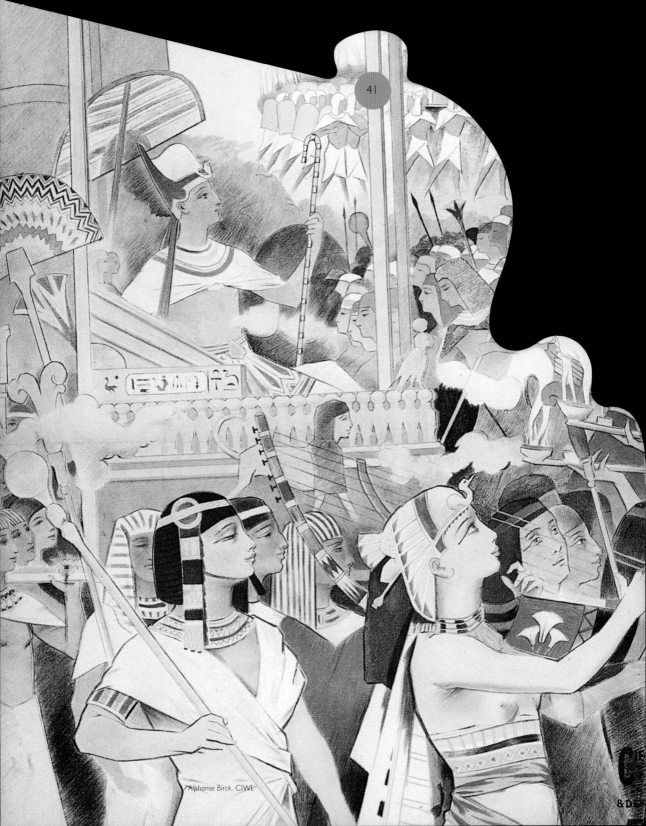

Alphonse Birck, CIWL

'The convoy set off. The two men stood at the window looking out at the long platform. The Orient Express was on the point of leaving on its three-day voyage across Europe.'

Agatha Christie

Jean de la Nézière, CIWL

Childhood memories also prompted historian Jean des Cars

to don the uniform of a Wagon-Lits guard and travel with the Orient Express. As a journalist, he attended a Compagnie des Wagons-Lits training course before boarding the train one evening in July 1974 and taking charge of Sleeping Car 3625 bound for Istanbul. 'Strangely enough, no-one ever seemed to query the designation Orient-Express or the entirely erroneous assumption that the train only ran in one direction, namely west to east. When one was headed for the Bosphorus, the name was entirely apposite. But when one was travelling back, the name seemed singularly inappropriate. I felt there was something distinctly odd about that'.

Rafael de Ochoa y Madrazo, CIWL

'What's the point if you don't ask questions of yourself, if you don't take a risk, try to win or lose, even at the risk of falling flat on your face?'

Louis Guilloux

Rafael de Ochoa y Madrazo, CIWL

I don't travel to go somewhere but for travel's own sake — I travel for the sheer pleasure of it. The important thing is to keep moving, to get to grips with the trials and tribulations of life.'
Robert Louis Stevenson

The same **might**
have been said of
similar trains

such as the 'Northern Express' or the 'Southern Express'. At least one inveterate east-west-east traveller took issue with these appellations: post-1918, the irresistible Elvire Popescu was the toast of Paris theatre-goers on account of her prodigious talent. 'You're right,' she said to me one day in that splendidly Central European accent of hers. 'When the train is on its way back to Paris, it should be known as the "Occident" Express'. Fair comment, I thought – except for the fact that her vowels tended to become somewhat distorted, the result being that it came out as 'Accident' Express!

Be that as it may, there appears little doubt that the Belgians and the French were more passionate about travelling east than were their eastern counterparts about travelling west …

'I've never been lucky
enough to miss a train
that ended up crashing.'
Jules Renard

> 'Travel broadens the mind.'
>
> Proverb

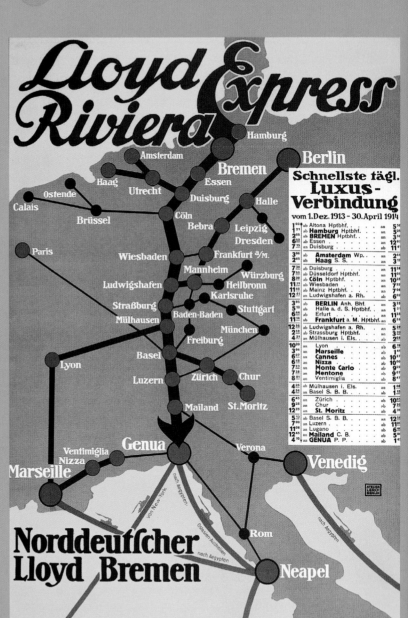

Rafael de Ochoa y Madrazo, CIWL

The best thing one can bring back from a voyage is oneself, safe and sound.

Persian proverb

'Some voyages seem set to illustrate life itself and can serve as symbols for existence. One makes the effort, one almost kills oneself at times trying to achieve something – and then one fails.'

Joseph Conrad

DR, PLM

'The mind is dulled by the routine of travel and even the most exotic and unusual places and extraordinary faces come to seem commonplace. But then the imagination awakes and one is suddenly struck by the strangeness of one's surroundings.'

Pierre Loti

SIMPLON·ORIENT·EXPRESS

ALEP

GRANDE BRETAGNE.FRANCE.SUISSE.ITALIE
SERBIE_CROATIE_SLOVENIE_BULGARIE
ROUMANIE_GRÈCE_TURQUIE_SYRIE

Jean de la Nézière, CIWL

'Parting is to die a
little,
To pine for what one
leaves.
One leaves a piece of
self behind
Always and everywhere.'
Edmond Haraucourt

It wasn't just children who **loved playing** with **trains**

– far from it. Ferdinand of Saxe-Coburg, who acceded to the title of Tsar of the Bulgars in 1908, was so obsessed by the Orient Express that he found it impossible to have the luxury train cross his lands without experiencing an insatiable urge to climb aboard. Totally au fait with the train's timetable, he would drive to the track and wait for it, instructing one of his aides to order the train to be stopped. Then, dressed in an outfit made to measure by a leading Parisian couturier, His Majesty would board the train and position himself between the driver and the engineer. He delighted in blowing the whistle and operating the steam pressure valve. Ignoring the discomfiture and protestations of the driver and engineer, Ferdinand would open the throttle, sending the Orient Express at hair-raising speed around tight bends, only to apply the brakes violently in order to 'monitor' the engine's performance. His intervention was not to the taste of the paying passengers or the buffet car personnel, who looked on in horror as sauce-boats were upended and cutlery and crockery flew this way and that. Meanwhile, back in the sleeping compartments, travellers would at best be jolted awake and at worst be tossed unceremoniously from their bunks. Ferdinand was unrepentant: the 120-tonne Orient Express was His Majesty's favourite toy …

Ferry de Nuit

COMPAGNIE INTERNATIONALE DE

Wagons-Lits directs vers Londres chaque nuit

pendant toute l'année au départ de Bruxelles (Midi)

Pour billets et reservations, s'adresser
aux chemins de fer Britanniques,
41, Boulevard Adolphe Max, Bruxelles.

SOUTHERN
BRITISH RAILWAYS

'A businessman needs
three umbrellas – one
for the office, one for
the home and one to
leave in the train.'
Paul Dickson

Complaints
accumulate

on Georges Nagelmackers' desk at the Compagnie Internationale – members of a royal household misbehave on board; an adviser to the king quotes the arrogant assertion of Romanian landowner Prince Bibesco to the effect that the Orient Express 'takes four hours to cross my land'. The Bulgarian sovereign regrets a series of 'incidents' and fervently hopes these will not lead to the Orient Express closing its routes to and across his country. But it is not all bad news, a monarch bestows a medal on Nagelmackers – albeit in exchange for an exceptional privilege, namely the right to hitch his private saloon carriage to the Orient Express as and when he sees fit …

LA HOLLANDE
LES CHAMPS DE FLEURS
SAISON MARS-MAI
PARCOUREZ LA HOLLANDE
avec des abonnements de 8 jours I°cl. fl. 28⁵⁰; II°cl. fl. 21⁷⁵; III°cl. fl. 15.

'The Dutch are so into cleanliness that they take a train to the country whenever they feel like spitting.'

Georges Courteline

Alesi d'Hugo, PLM

'The best that can
happen en route is that
you get lost. When you
do, all your planning
is irrelevant and that's
when the real journey
begins ...'
          Nicolas Bouvier

Alesi d'Hugo, PLM

'Nothing is more beautiful than the moment the journey is about to begin, that instant when tomorrow's horizon holds out such promise.'

Milan Kundera

ELEKTR.STRASSENBAHNEN
IM KANTON ZUG (SCHWEIZ)

'We discover our true
self not in some resort or
other, but on the road,
in the towns, as one of
a crowd, as one thing
among many, as a man
among men.'

Jean-Paul Sartre

'Coming home, like
going away, exudes its
own peculiar sadness.'

Gustave Flaubert

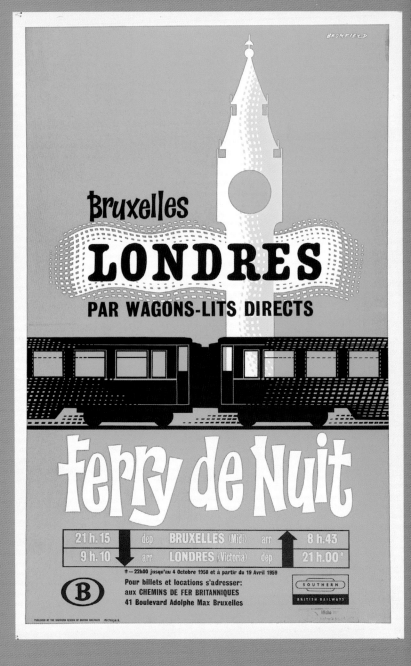

savignac

voyagez sans risque...

**TRAINS AUTOS COUCHETTES
SERVICES AUTOS EXPRESS**

SNCF

'I sometimes feel that
I'm travelling the world
aimlessly in order to
collect material for
future nostalgia.'
Vikram Seth

Raymond Savignac, © ADAGP Paris 2005

On **11 November, 1918,**

La Compagnie Internationale des
WAGONS-LITS
vous souhaite

BONNE NUIT
LE CONFORT DES WAGONS-LITS

BON APPÉTIT
WAGONS-RESTAURANTS-BUFFETS-BARS-RESTAURANTS D'AÉROPORTS

BON VOYAGE
400 AGENCES DE VOYAGES

Guy Georget

Guy Georget, CIWL

restaurant car 2419 of the Compagnie des Wagons-Lits was converted to serve as field headquarters for Ferdinand Foch, Marshal of France. And it was there, in a railway cutting at Rethondes near Compiègne, that the commander of the French forces formally received the German delegation sent to conclude the Armistice Agreement that heralded the end of the First World War. Over two decades later, on 22 June, 1940, a triumphant Adolf Hitler sat in that selfsame carriage in Rethondes to accept the humiliating surrender of the French Army. At a stroke of the pen, the Führer also signed the virtual death warrant of Europe's luxury express train services.

Valerio Adami, CIWL

'Travel teaches
tolerance.'
Benjamin Disraeli

'A traveller is a historian of sorts, whose duty it is to recount faithfully what he has seen or heard. He should neither invent nor omit.'

François René de Chateaubriand

The **Orient Express**
was mothballed

during the so-called 'Phoney War' of September 1939 to June 1940, although its younger sibling, the Simplon-Orient Express, continued to circulate with all the trappings of pre-war luxury. One branch of the Simplon-Orient served Athens, the other Istanbul but, in Belgrade, the train took on several carriages from Berlin in what was clearly a flagrant abuse of Yugoslavia's officially neutral status. In March 1942, however, the Simplon-Orient Express was itself taken out of service and its network dismantled, although a reduced service continued to operate between Sofia and Istanbul under German authority and supervision.

'There are as many
possible journeys as
there are leaves on the
traveller's tree.'
Kenneth White

The **National Socialist** regime maintained an **ersatz** Orient Express service

between Berlin and Istanbul. One regular traveller on the route was German ambassador Franz van Papen, who directed secret service operations on behalf of the Reich from his base in Ankara.

The *Cicero*
Affair,

a novel by L.C. Moyzisch, which was published by Julliard in Paris in 1951 and adapted for the cinema the following year (*Five Fingers* directed by Joseph L. Mankiewicz), is a true story of the twilight world of espionage set against the atmospheric backdrop of the Second World War.

*Important things happen
not at one's destination
but along the way to it.'
Milorad Pavic*

'One never goes as
far as when one does
not know where one is
going.'
Christopher Columbus

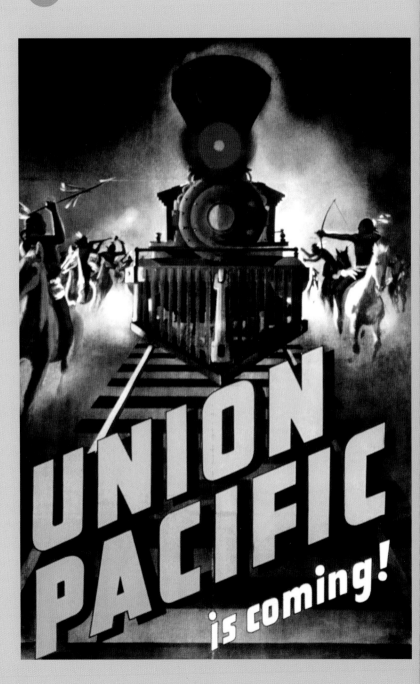

*'We do not take a trip,
the trip takes us; it
takes us apart and puts
us back together again.'*
David Le Breton

Luxury
train advertising

in the first half of the nineteenth century was not confined to stark posters designed to communicate basic timetable information. This typical example features a call to general mobilisation, symbolised by the two small *tricolore* flags.

Vivent les Vacances   *Au revoir Paris*   *Aquarelle de Léo Fontan*

Gustav Krollmann

Colour lithography

pioneer, Jules Chéret, was a key player in efforts by the railways to encourage luxury train travel to prominent tourist destinations and to extol the riches of Europe's cultural heritage. The train poster was born and with it came kitsch and enticing images of landscapes and cityscapes designed to lure the traveller in quest of exciting new destinations. Over time, the poster genre quickly evolved in line with prevalent artistic tastes, attracting the likes of Roger Broders, Albert Brenet, Pierre Fix-Masseau, Hervé Moran, Paul Colin, Charles Loupot, Jean Carlu, Bernard Villemot, A.M. Cassandre, André François, Raymond Savignac and others, not to mention leading latter-day artists such as Salvador Dali and Georges Mathieu. Each in his own way celebrated the charms of travelling by rail, complementing hard information such as timetables and tariffs with images of speed, comfort and safety. The message was often accompanied by frequent injections of wit and humour …

P.L.M

St HONORÉ LES BAINS (NIÈVRE)

IMP. F. CHAMPENOIS. 66, Boul¹ S¹ Michel - PARIS.

Louis Tauzin, PLM

'Shouldn't we protest against the waste of space between two sets of rails?'

Marcel Duchamp

'We travel the world in
search of something and
come home to find it.'
George Moore

Cussotti, PLM

'The real voyage is the outward voyage. Once you arrive, the voyage is over. Today, people start at the end and work back.'

Hugo Verlomme

'The real voyage of
discovery does not consist
in looking for new
landscapes but looking
at the old through fresh
eyes.'

Marcel Proust

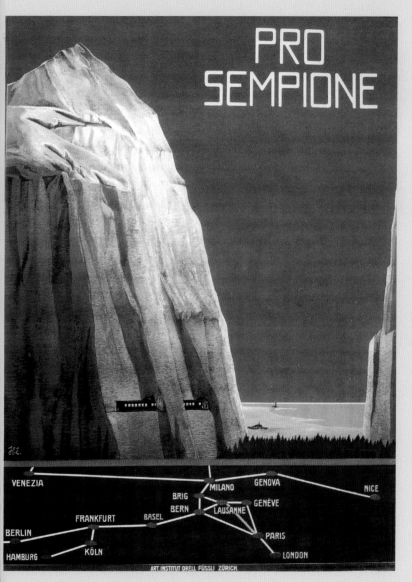

'Travel doesn't foster understanding but it does condition the eye to see the world in a new light.'

Italo Calvino

In the period between the two World Wars,

poster advertising became less anecdotal. A.M. Cassandre (1901–1968) was in the vanguard of a golden age of graphics, and his posters for international sleeper and Pullman services are now acknowledged as veritable masterpieces.

'Oh, Thomas Cook &
Son, who make travel
easy with those long
ribbon-like tickets filed
away in plastic wallets,
what fateful spell did
you cast on 20th century
people?'

John Dos Passos

Mouron Cassandre. CIWL.

Cassandre's

articulate poster work elevated luxury train voyage advertising to new heights, conferring a sense of aristocratic distinction via his resolutely abstract images that deliberately excluded locomotives and carriages in favour of rendering the essence of train travel. *Nord-Express*, *l'Oiseau Bleu*, *l'Etoile du Nord* and *Wagon-Bar* are stunning examples of his ability to capture in graphic form his personal vision of train travel as an escape from mundane everyday life. His poster for the launch of economy-class sleeper services, for example, is masterful: a red signal light shining on the tracks in the middle of the night reinforces the notion of safety and comfort, reassuring the traveller that his only concern is to sleep away the hours, safely cocooned in his couchette.

'To travel is to demand
immediately what time
can only offer us little
by little.'

Paul Morand

**VITESSE
EXACTITUDE
CONFORT**

SOCIÉTÉ NATIONALE DES CHEMINS DE FER FRANÇAIS

Mastering
the subject

French poster artist, Adolphe Jean Marie Mouron Cassandre, approached his texts with the same precision he adopted in his graphics. The meticulously-worded text of his revolutionary 1938 poster of Charles Peignot, silent partner in the famous *Deberny et Peignot* typesetting foundries, is designed to preclude subsequent litigation between artist and client.

'Travel would be a fine thing if only it didn't mean getting up so early in the morning.'

Jean de la Fontaine

True to **type**

Cassandre was always alert to the importance of the accompanying text, which underpinned the image and ideally enhanced it. With precious few exceptions, his railway posters always carried text. Each poster is a virtuoso display of harmonious line and colour, reminiscent of composer Arthur Honegger's powerfully-evocative symphony, *Pacific 123*.

'Most travel is
interesting in terms of
what we anticipate and
what we remember, with
the real world being
reduced to losing our
luggage.'

Regina Nadelson

Maurice Toussaint, © ADAGP Paris 2005

VERS LE MONT. BLANC

'One should travel not
to lose oneself – which
is impossible – but to
find oneself.'

Jean Grenier

'The most important thing about travel is the traveller.'

André Suarès

Bernard Villemot, © ADAGP Paris 2005

Nothing

is more appealing than

the prospect of travelling by train. A train ticket is the open sesame to a magic-carpet ride.

The voyage beckons from the moment one sets foot on the platform.

The journey begins as soon as the traveller enters the carriage.

Departing by train is a sure-fire guarantee of getting away from it all.

The first clickety-clack as the train moves off …

In this era of high-speed trains that whisk us from one destination to another in double-quick time, Jean-Paul Caracalla invites us to pause for a moment to consider the halcyon days of rail travel. Caracalla, travel writer, train enthusiast and erstwhile Wagon Lits employee, takes us on a breathtaking poster journey that more than rivals any we have ever experienced in the hustle and bustle of 21st century transport.

Poster art – and the extraordinary talent of artists such as Chéret, Brenet, Villemot, Loupot, Savignac, Morvan, François and even the great Salvador Dali – exerts a fascination all of its own, imparting a deeper meaning and a heightened aesthetic to what, when all is said and done, was originally no more than advertising, plain and simple.

As these pages unfold, we embark on an extended voyage across time and talent in the company of writers and aesthetes such as Morand, Larbaud, Nabokov, Claudel and other inveterate train travellers, whose often acerbic observations transport us with a snap of the fingers to exotic destinations: Venice, Tashkent, Samarkand …

Through the eyes of these elegant and eloquent travelling companions, we experience the express train as a synonym of luxury and sensual pleasure, its mahogany-panelled sleeping cars in every sense a 'moving passport' across Europe by night.

An incomparably sweet nostalgia redolent of leather and burnished copper, immaculate linen, panama hats and frosted glass windows bearing the initials W.L. sweeps over us as we travel sedately through the countryside.

But our journey is not over. We can embark on it repeatedly in the pages of this volume, remembering only to stand back as the doors close automatically on a bygone age of travel.

L. M.

506—Santa Fe's "Super Chief" Traveling thru the Orange Groves, California

© CURT TEICH & CO., INC.　　　　　　　　　　　　　　　　　　　　　　　0B-H678

photographic credits

© **ADAGP Paris 2005** *Roger Broders 30 – Michael Druck 20-21 – Pierre Fix Masseau 4, 13, 21, 36 – Dorival Geo 91 – Franck H. Mason 14 – Raymond Savignac 63 – Jacques Touchet 8 – Maurice Toussaint 90 – Bernard Villemot 34, 35, 93.*

A.K.G images *Michael Druck 20-21 – Pierre Fix Masseau 4, 7 – Herbert Kapitzki 88, 89 – Franck H. Mason 14 – DR 25, 33, 68.*

Bridgeman Art Library *Philippe Noyer 66.*

Bridgeman Art Library/Archives Charmet *DR 73.*

CIWL *Valerio Adami 65 – Charles Alo 23 – Alphonse Birck 41 – W. S. Bylitipolos 31 – Mouron Cassandre 84 – Pierre-Fix Masseau 13, 21 – Guy Georget 64 – Jean de la Nézière 42, 53 – Rafael de Ochoa y Madrazo 10, 29, 44, 45, 49 – Jacques Touchet 8 – DR 24, 38.*

Collection Galdoc-Grob/Kharbine Tapabor *Alesi d'Hugo 58 – L. Symonnot 80 – Maurice Toussaint 90 – DR 9, 30, 57.*

Collection IM/Kharbine Tapabor *Louis Tauzin 77 – DR 37, 50, 51.*

Collection Kharbine Tapabor *Henri Folart 16 – Leo Fontan 74 – Jean de la Nézière 53 – DR 17, 21, 38, 53, 60, 61, 81, 83.*

Collection Perrin/Kharbine Tapabor *Albert Brenet 86 – Pierre Fix Masseau 36 – Dorival Geo 91 – A. Nivault 27 – Raymond Savignac 63 – Eric 92 – Bernard Villemot 93 – DR 24.*

Corbis Lake County Museum *95.*

Corbis Swin Ink *Daniel Buzzi 19 – W. S. Bylitipolo 18 – Cussotti 79 – Henri Gray 78 – Alesi d'Hugo 59 – Gustav Krollmann 75 – Grif Teller 47 – DR 59.*

Jürgen Klein *Valerio Adami 65 – Charles Alo 23 – Alphonse Birck 41 – Bromfield 62 – W. S Bylitipolos 31 – Mouron Cassandre 84 – P. V. Dullous 55 – Pierre-Fix Masseau 13 – Guy Georget 64 – P. Gewis 40, 48 – Jean de la Nézière 42 – Rafael de Ochoa y Madrazo 10, 29, 44, 45, 49 – Jacques Touchet 8 – Bernard Villemot 34, 35.*

PLM *Roger Broders 30 – Cussotti 79 – Henri Folart 16 – Dorival Geo 91 – Alesi d'Hugo 58, 59 – Louis Tauzin 77 – DR 52.*

Rue des Archives *73.*

Rue des Archives/Tallandier *70, 71.*

© **Mouron Cassandre** *84*

Compagnie des Wagons-Lits, PLM, its names, logos and records are the copyright and trade mark properties of the group ACCOR © TM

Every effort has been made to obtain the necessary permissions.
Any errors or omissions made known to us will be corrected in the next edition.